PIOUS REFLECTIONS,

AND

DEVOVT PRAYERS,

ON

SEVERAL POINTS

OF

FAITH AND MORALITY,

FROM MAN'S CREATION

TO HIS CONSUMMATION.

By the very Reverend Father NICOLAS of the holy Crofs, Exprovincial of the English Recollects, and Chapelain in ordinary to her Majefty of great Britain.

DOWAY, By M. MAIRESSE

M. DC. XCV.

This scarce antiquarian book is included in our special *Legacy Reprint Series*. In the interest of creating a more extensive selection of rare historical book reprints, we have chosen to reproduce this title even though it may possibly have occasional imperfections such as missing and blurred pages, missing text, poor pictures, markings, dark backgrounds and other reproduction issues beyond our control. Because this work is culturally important, we have made it available as a part of our commitment to protecting, preserving and promoting the world's literature.

TO HER MOST
EXCELLENT MAJESTY,
MARY
QUEEN OF GREAT BRITAIN &c.

ADAM,

The great Apostle saint Iames, declares that al our blessings of nature, grace, or Glory, descend from above from the father of light, in whom is found no shadow of vicissitude, or change: that we can lay no offerings upon our Altars which

have not parted from his hands;
in fine, that we can give him nothing that his not of his own. Yet
there is one thing, and that alone
we can cal ours, which is gratitude,
and that only God expects from us,
because tis a voice which loudly proclaims our dependency, and his
greatnes.

Now, Madam, sovraign
Princes are in the next degree of obliging their subjects: first we ow
unto them the duty of observance
and obedience, which exact a great
part of vvhat vve have, or can do,
as tributary to their Dignity; next,
when they are pleased to superadd
any liberality of their own, it renders us so uncapable of a return,
that we find a necessity of having

recours to our propriety of nature as rational, which is gratitude: for the Eminence of a Benefactor adds much to the value of the gift, and cōsequently to aspire to a compensation is a kind of presumption in a subject to his soveraign.

Saint Thomas in his rules of gratitude prescribes that after our discharg of thanks, honor, and respect to our Benefactor, we ought to make a return, if not proportionable to the gift received, at least to the utmost of our ability: hence wil appear to your Majesty my poor condition, that after al the acknowledgments that can issue from a grateful heart for your unprizable favours, after al the testimonies of submission, and veneration due to your greatnes, and

Now, MADAM, *Providence having so ordaind, that it came out of the press, a little before that auspicious day which disclosed unto us a glorious sun, our hopeful Prince of wales, who revives the almost wither'd hopes of al your true subjects, and makes them blossom forth anew, I say this pleasing reflection made me venture to present to your Majesty on that blessed day, together with these, a hymn of thanksgiving for that pretious gift, in whom is comprised (after your Royal Consort) al we can expect of happines to our unfortunate Country; and I hope also this powerful attractive may invite your Majesty the more frequently to take into your hands these poor fragments of devotion. Thus vvith al humility, and in al duty I subscribe*

YOUR MAJESTY'S,

Most obedient Subject, devoted Orator, and Chaplain unworthy.

B. NICOLAS of the holy Cross.

for, either temporal, or spiritual, are the effects of your benign influences. Now whilst we enumerate these your liberalities, ô Blessed Trinity, it were high ingratitude to pass over in silence this Choice one of your inexhausted bounty; to wit, our hopeful Prince of Wales; whom we acknowledg to be your munificent gift, and therefore permit us to lay him at the foot of your sacred Altar, and from thence convey unto your supream Majesty the perfumes of praise and thanksgiving; that on this day of your great solemnity, a son is born unto us, design'd we hope by your al-powerful hand to be a

Prince of peace; to settle our unfortunate distracted Nation, which for many late years past has by a strange stupidity obstructed your mercy and its own happines. Next our humble petition in his behalf is, that when the Crown (of which he is heir apparent) shal be due to him, he may quietly enter into possession: Then may he be inspired to shelter his three Kingdoms under the patronage of you, ô August Trinity, and that his power of Majesty may equally sway in al his Dominions. Give him wisdom likewise to govern according to your Holy laws: give him a heart of Iustice, to reward merit, and punish offenders by this means may he purchase to himself the love and fear of his people, the tvvo main pillars of a Crovvn. Lastly, after a happy raign, and a life attempered with al Christian and Princely vertues, may he exchange an earthly Crown, for one Celestial.

Amen.

A HYMN

On the birth of his Royal Highnes

THE PRINCE OF WALES,

The hopes of our Crown, and the Crown of our hopes.

Quis putas puer iste erit? Luc. 1.

GReat God, whose al-wise Providence,
Is the Prime Mobile from whence
 At Human Action flows:
But with a more endearing Love,
With a peculiar care above,
 Does Kings and Crowns dispose.
Accept the Tribute of the praise,
Which every loyal subject pays,
 At this most happy hour,
When all-propitious Heaven did smile,
And signal Bleßings on our Ile
 Did prodigally pour.
When you a kind of Saviour sent:
A Prince, our longing Heart's content:
 A favour undeserv'd:

A Prince by Providence conceiv'd,
By Wonder from the grave retriev'd,
      By Miracle preserv'd:
Sure, gracious God, this shou'd presage,
He'll be the Phænix of the Age;
      England's Redemption's near;
Since James and JESUS so agree,
Since 'twixt 'em such affinity
      Does hitherto appear.
As JESUS in his Crib was crost,
As JESUS here and there was tost,
      And so to glory past:
O may our hope's reviver too,
From suff'ring to his glory go,
      And so be crown'd at last.
To fit him for this great design,
Give him, Good God, a soul divine,
      A brave heroick heart:
May graces al concenter there,
Vertue and Valour co-insphere;
      The nation to convert.
So into Hymns the noise of wars;
Lightning of Cannons into stars,
      Wil soon converted be;
      To Pearls our tears,
      To Joys our fears,
      And ev'ry soul to thee.
      Amen.

THE PROEM.

WHEN I consider (O my God) those infinit mercies you have bestowd on me the most unworthy of your creatures, I confes it puts me to a stand; so far they surpas any return I can make: however, I resolue not to be staind with the guilt of ingratitude: wherefore for every benefit of yours, which are as so many testimonies of

(2)

your Love, I present you with as many thanks from a grateful heart: and since by no obsequiousnes of mine, I can reach to a ful compensation, I wil at least return love for love.

I. A MEDITATION

ON THE BENEFITS OF MANS CREATION.

Consider that God, amidst a mass of creatures he designed to make happy, was pleased to draw me out of nothing, and give me a being: next, that his sovereign power left Millions of creatures in their nothing, at the same time he gave me being; who deserv'd it no more than they; so that it was a pure effect of his kindness in preferring me before them. Again, he not only confer'd on me a simple being, but an eternal one, which should never perish; a being indow'd with reason, and Ennobling this my being with knowledg, with liberty, and with a Law; that I might know my Creator, that with a free wil I might acknowledg my dependance on him, and receive his commands: lastly, that I might be the more easily induc'd to pay him the just tribute of obedience; he subjected al the creatures of this inferior world to mans Dominion: nay fram'd the sun, moon, and those celestial bodies, for his use and convenience. Hence I consider the eminent dignity of man, that was constituted Lord and master of the univers; Lions and Tigers were aw'd at the majesty of his looks; al other creatures at his beck, and giuing to every one its name conformable to its nature: by which it appears how perfectly he knew their proprieties and inftincts, so the better to manage them to the end for which they were created. No storms or tempests, nothing in disorder while he preserv'd his innocence: al the seasons of the year kind and suitable to their productions; no malignant vapors to blast a fresh complexion; al things conspiring to deliciate his senses.

REFLEXION.

The necessity of grace.

THe gift of creation is highly to be valued, and justly merits our acts of gratitude; but that of conservation seems to lay a greater obligation upon us, because it is a favour without intermission: for creation is but one act in our Maker, whereas Conservation is a production repeated as it were every moment. The like is requisit also in the being of grace, for without a continual supply of that supernatural quality, we presently slip back into sin. Hence the condition of Man seems very deplorable, when on the one side we cōsider his tye of a cōstant gratitude for the creation, and cōservation both of nature and grace, and on the other, his weaknes and imbecility to perform what is good. The sacred text abundantly sets forth this inability; affirming that we can not frame a good thought, nay not so much as desire to do it without the grace of God. Saint Austin says none can move towards their Salvation, without God inviting; that none invited can effect any thing without God assisting; lastly, he asists none to carry on their good works to the end, unless sued to, by an humble supplication.

As to the first, that is exciting grace, he offers it to al : for he enlightens al men who enter in to the world. As to sanctifying grace, he bestovvs it where he finds a disposition on our side to receive it : for nature teaches that forms are not introduc'd but into subjects dispos'd for them : the soul of a beast informs not the trunck of a tree, nor a rational soul the body of a beast , because their is no disposition in the matter : so grace, being a supernatural form, enters not in to a soul unprepar'd for it.

The remote dispositions unto grace are moral acts of virtue, as to give to every one what is his due: to relieve the distressed out of a natural compassion of their miseries: or when a sinner prays to be freed from his sins without doing any thing more to the effect of his prayer.

The immediate disposition unto grace is usualy reduced to the three Theological Vertues; Faith, Hope, and Charity, or Contrition: by Faith we captivate our understanding, and our Reason to the obedience of reveal'd truths; so that faith is the begining and Basis of our salvation. Hope rises to the expectation of eternal felicity, by the means of grace (Which is gratis given) and good works; for could we attain to our Salvation by the strength of our natural faculties, a Redeemer had been to us unnecessary; Fear, humility, Prayer, thanksgiving, and a sense of divine mercy, would have found no admittance in our presumptious minds: wherefore God has decreed, not to part with the pretious gift of grace unles we do him the honor to expect it from his hands, and perform somthing on our part. Charity unites us to God by a love of Benevolence, rendring delightful to us what is so to him, as also displeasing what is distastful to him: so that we are carryed on to contrition by a motive of charity which may justly be termd a loving dolor, or a dolorous Love. To conclude, our salvation depends on God and our selves; let us play our part and we are secure. That God requires our cooperation is an effect of his goodnes, for vvhilst we dispose our selves by our own actions he makes us as it vvere partners vvith him: by this means our supream felicity is derived unto us in the most noble vvay of purchase, that is, by the cooperation of our free vvil, joyned vvith the principal cause of our justification, vvhich is Gods love and mercy.

As for its final effects of perseverance he only expects vve should ask; and can there be any thing more indulgent then to fee a hand open to give, if vve vvil but open our lips to demand. Novv in this laft requifit, our unfortunate parent Adam vvas deficient, for trufting to his ovvn condition, vvhich appeard fo happy as to vvant nothing but his confummated felicity, behold him left to himfelf: and then vvhat fucceeded? he began to difdain to keep the garden of another, he vvould be a Proprietor, and be like unto God; hence immediatly he was difpoyled of his pofeffions, thrown out of

Paradife, difturbed by rebellious paffions, clouds caft over his underftanding, which depriv'd him of the fpecious rays of knowledg which God had given him ; naked, becaufe ftript of the vefture of innocence : poor, having forfeited with his innocence al his treafures and fovereignty. O how the fcene is changed ! how difaftrous are the effects of fin! by this fad example we may learn the neceffity of preferving grace : for if in heaven and Paradife this was requifit, much more ought we who are weakned by the venom of original fin, fear the want of this conftant ftream of grace :

We may therefore conclude, it is our part to vvork our Salvation vvith fear and trembling, Saint Paul assuring vve can not perform the least good act unless begun, held on, and perfected (so as to render it meritorious) vvithout the assisting grace of God.

Spiritual masters proscribe two principal expedients by vvhich vve may preserve our selves in the state of grace: the one is prayer, vvhose povver is such, that could the treasury of God be exhausted, prayer vvould do it; for Christ our Lord hath engaged his vvord never to deny vvhat is demanded by fervent prayer. Nay

S. Chrisostom says that God hoards up blessings for us, and expects only our petition to deliver them out: as if Iustice obliged him by virtue of his promise to accord vvhat vve ask. Nay it has not only povver to dravv from him blessings, but likevvise to tye up his hands that he inflict not iust punishments upon offenders: hovv svveetly did God expostulate vvith Moyses that hee should cease to pray: and vvhy? because he might have liberty to fal heavy upon his ungrateful people. Novv vvhilst vve read those vvonders, is it not a greater vvonder hovv man comes to be miserable, hovv he can grudg thanks for his creation and shamefully sink from a state of grace, having such a povverful engin, as that of prayer, to settle, and secure to him his final end.

But to take off som part of our admiration, you must know this irresistable effect of prayer is annex'd to certain conditions, without vvhich God lends not his ear to our supplications; tho they appear never so humble and earnest: if the first is, it must be for somthing that conduces to salvation: next, it must issue from pure lips, and from a heart innocent, and unstain'd vvith sin. the last is, that vve perfectly
for-

forgive our enemies, as we desire God should forgive us: if any of these be wanting it may evacuate the force of prayer, and render it ineffectual.

The next expedient is to avoid dangerous occasions of sin: We posses our treasure in brittle caskets; one wanton glance, or amorous expression, hath oft wrought a flaw in the cristal innocence of persons who were looked upon like Cedars eminent in vertue and sanctity. Wherefore if we prove so happy as to be restored to grace by participation of the Sacraments, tho our wounds be closed up, yet remember our enemies are not so quel'd, but they may rally, and make another attempt: our passions, and il habits have not so given up al their right to reason and piety, as to secure us from a second revolt and mutiny: no, no, we ought to live in a continual distrust of our selves, we ought to hold pretious the least degree of grace, since it is steeped in the bloud of JESUS-CHRIST; a flower produced of a thorn from his head, and a balm composed of his sweat and tears. It vvas the sense of mans frailties that occasioned ye great servants of God to shrowd themselves into deserts, and little cells, that they might not expose unto hazard, and render fruitless the ineftimable benefits of our creation, confervation and redemption; let us remember then the caution our Bleffed Saviour gave to his Difciples, that whilft they enjoyed light, they should preferve themfelves in light; that is in grace, for fo they might be enabled to break throu the mifts of fin which involue them in the darknefs of ingratitude and preferve to themfelves the happy title of being the fons of light.

THE PRAYER.

Divine artist, who hast framed man to your own Image and likeness, and designed him for supream felicity, yet with a continual dependance on the exhibition of your graces: and this doubtless out of an endearing providence: that whilst by our prayers we draw your blessings upon us, we at the same time might be mindful of the hand from whence they parted: grant, we beseech you, that in rendring constant acts of gratitude we may not only preserve your favours, but also encrease them: until richly laden with merits we arrive at the land of Promise where we are to receive the last

Broaks of your immense love in Eternal beatitude. Amen.

II. THE BENEFITS OF THE SACRAMENTS, ESPECIALY OF PENNANCE.

After the shipvvrack of Adam, our great and good God vvas stil pleased to retain the bovvels of compassion, and resentment of love tovvards his unfortunate children. Wherefore in the plenitude of time he sent his only son to pay our ransom, and restore us to the right of our lost inheritance: novv as his providential care had allotted remedies for our corporal infirmities, no less vvas he solicitous to provide against the vvounds vve might receive by sin throu the vveaknes of our nature impaired by an original stain: to this end he instituted the Sacram. vvhich should smooth unto us the vvay of salvation, and be as certain aqueducts to convey the merits and graces he has purchased for us by his pretious blood and passion: and since Christ came to enact a lavv of grace he reserv'd the institution of such Sacraments as confer an inherent Sanctity, until his coming, as the most seasonable time both to Issue forth the testimonies of his love and mercy, as also to releive poor man so fastned to earth, that without great difficulty he could not apply himself to works of piety in that degree as to attain unto grace: but we wil here in pattitular consider the Sacrament of Pennance usualy stiled the second plank after shipwrack, together with the difficulties that occur in the performance, as also the benefits arising from thence, so to counterballance the apprehended rigors which attend it.

REFLEXION.

The comfort of Confession.

Vertue has this happy circumstance annexed unto it, that the face of difficulties affright not, nay rather it begets a greater animosity, like to the sight of bloud which adds rage to Elephants: the reason is, where there is more of hardship, there is more of merit. In the civil law to conceal a conspiracy against the King or commonwealth, thô to preserve a friend, a near relation, nay even a Parent, is esteem'd petty treason; but at the tribunal of Pennance to conceal a mortal trespas is an act of high treason, and the punishment decreed for it, beyond that of drawing and quartering.

The first essential part of this Sacrament is sorrow, which disposes for pardon. Now the sorrow which is absolutely necessary, and no less will suffice, is called attrition: it springs from an apprehension of eternal punishment, or privation of eternal glory: and albeit this implies our own interest, yet there is intermingled with it a fear of being set at perpetual enmity with God, or of incurring the loss of enjoying him in whom is compris'd the felicity of Saints: both which suppose a knowledg of God by an act of faith, which is a gift of the Holy Ghost; representing the horrors of Hel, and the happines of Heaven. Observe likewise, that no sorrow which is purely natural can reach (tho joyn'd with the Sacrament) to the remission of sin, because the Holy Ghost, who alone is the source of al Sanctification, does not work there.

Next, you are to know that this sorrow implies a firm purpose never to relaps: and this firm purpose includes the avoiding al imminent dangers of sin, without which the purpose is trifling, and as it were none : it is like (says Saint Bonaventure) one that resolues no more to be burnt, yet stil walks amidst flames: hence it is that many persever in their wicked ways notwithstanding they frequent this Sacrament; while they dally with occasions of sin, and yet hope to continue innocent; a thing as possible as to be always handling pitch, and never dawb our fingers.

The second essential part of pennance is confession, a remedy that seems bitter, and bears the face of severity : for nothing is more repugnant to nature then to betray ones self; yet to this we are obliged in this Sacrament how then can it be a blessing when so severe? the reason is, because it leads us to perform heroick acts of vertue; as to overcom our selves, which is a greater victory then that of Lions : it puts us upon the task of knowing our selves, which is the highest science; for there is not a puff of vanity within us, a grain of Pride, a spark of concupiscence, envy, revenge, or the like, but must be sifted, and layd open; and thô this be harsh to sense, it is not so to reason, that considers the exuberant fruits which countervail the struglings of nature. What large promises were made to Abraham for his obedience to Sacrifice his son? A penitent doth more; he sacrifices his shame and bashfulnes, his strong inclination to hide his imperfections: in a word, he becomes a perfect Holocaust, accusing himself to be a sinner, which is to say, a moral nothing; nay he is carried on so far as to acknowledg that which al men abhor, that is, to be ungrateful; Many have been content to bear the character of other crimes, but to be an ingrate is a monster in nature, and no vvhere found to be ovvnd, or acknovvleg'd, but in the Sacrament of pennance. Wherefore if selfdenyal sets a value upon good works, tis no where practi‑ sed so to the life as in Confes‑ sion; and consequently selflove is subdued, which is a great step to perfection; hence you see that to fit our selves for the due discharg of Confession, we are excited to the most generous acts of Christian ver‑ tues, as humility, selfdenyal, and a perfect survey of our own misery.

Besides, if you consider with an unbyasd understanding the laying open of your most se‑ cret defects in this Sacrament, you wil find no such horror as you imagin; nay tis a great relief in any disaster: for when overpresd with any affliction (abstracting) from any divine precept) what a comfort it is to have a freind to whom I can securely unbreast my self, and dilate upon my aggrievances? and thô he can afford me no remedy, yet tis an ease to discours of my misfortunes with him: how much more Consolatory is it then, when charged with sin, to fly to the sanctuary of this Sacrament, where I find the securest repository of my great concern, a friendship above al the most disinteressed; that is, a person employ'd by Heaven, whose office is to Compassionate my condition, to imprint in me a horror of my crimes, and after pious instructions for future prevention, has power to give me an act of oblivion for al that is past, supposing a sincere repentance, and a firm purpose never to relaps.

Hence I wonder not on great solemnities to behold Confessionals beset with Penitents, al pressing for audience, that their misdeeds may be raz'd out from the eternal book of accounts, and they return lightsom, enrich'd with a new being, more prizable then a human, nay Angelical being, precisely considered in the Order of nature: I say to behold this passionate crowding to be disburthen'd of their sins,
were

were enough methinks to convince, that it can not be the effect of policy, but must needs issue from a divine power and institution.

Satisfaction is the finishing part of pennance: for the sin, or guilt, is taken away before, by vertue of the other precedent parts; as also the eternal punishment due to sin is exchanged into a temporal satisfaction, which is sacramental, enjoyn'd by the Priest, besides what the penitent does of his own accord by fasting, prayer, alms, or any work of piety; it contributes likewise to compleat this sacrifice of justice: so Saint Ambrose terms it; for 'tis just that reparation should be made of Gods honour taken away by sin, and as by unlawful pleasures we have trespassed against his holy commands; so in our persons tis fit we feel the smart of our misdeeds.

After this Anatomy of pennance, let us see what advantages accrue to a penitent, and whether they may not justly be put into the ballance with the bitter ingredients whereof it is compos'd.

First we are taught by faith that this sacrament, perform'd vith al due circumstances, enriches us with sanctifying grace which sin had destroyd in us;

so that of sinners we becom just. It is true we approach like slaves laden with chains, but tis to the end they may be filed off: we approach as enemies to God, but with hopes to return his friends, reconciled to the eternal Father, by the merits of Christ's death and Passion, whose pretious bloud trickles down upon us throû the Conduit of this reviving Sacrament.

The next effect of pennance is, that by the remission of sin, those acts of vertue which in themselves were good, but withered and blasted while deprived of grace, do recouer their verdure, and spring forth into merit whenfoever a foul is reconciled to God by this facrament of pennance.

Laftly, it enlivens the expiring foul to that height that she feems even to have gain'd by her fatal blow: Cardinal Hugo giving to it in fom confideration a prerogative beyond that of innocence: fo much the loft sheep is valued, that acknowledging his fault and promifing amendment is born on the shepherds shoulders, as if in preference to the other ninety nine. For there is nothing more knotty then to break the chains of vice, and pafs into the freedom of vertue: becaufe man is hamperd in the allurements of ye flesh, in ye nets of the world, and the wiles of Satan; so that to extricate himself from these engagements, and pass from vice to vertue is in som sense more then never to have known what sin is: as Saint Ambrose says, the memory to have fallen from justice wil render a penitent more ambitious to raise himself in the way of Iustice and Piety.

How justly then may this Sacrament be termd a recreation or gift of a new being, more prizable then that of our Creation which cost Almighty God only but one word, one single *Fiat*, while this other was not purchased but at the rate of his bitter death and passion. Wherefore you ought never to approach to this Tribunal without an humble acknowledgment of mercy, and immortal thanks for the supernatural production of grace, the greatest of benefits derived unto us by this Sacrament.

THE PRAYER.

O God, I adore your wisdom, which by an admirable contrivance has so dispensed your liberalities in this sacrament of penance as to oblige us to search into the depth, and nature of our wounds by sin, that being conscious of the danger it might render us the more solicitous to seek a remedy, and becom the more grateful for the cure: I adore no leſs your goodnes in prescribing such ingredients, as being exactly prepared wil not only set us right in our claims to your Kingdom, but also Encrease our treasures there: Grant therefore, I beseech you, that approaching to this Holy sacrament, my love may be disinteressed; the account of my failings made without disguise, and my returns for what I ow compleatly just: this done, I claim your sacred promise that the pardon I receive here, may be ratified in Heaven. Amen.

III. THE BENEFIT OF AFFLICTION.

Let us consider the nature of a Benefit which consists either in the preservation from som Evil, or in the collation of som good, and this either at present, or by certain means to lead us to it: now this definition very aptly quadrates with afflictions; for adversity gives check to the most part of those vices incident to mankind: ad is the securest clue to guide us to our final end and soveraign good. Whereas on the contrary, Prosperity draws us from the practise of vertue, carries us on to pleasures, and a neglect of our duty to God: stifling in us al remembrance we ow to the author of our Being. David, whilst under the persecution of Saul, was a man according to Gods own heart, but when victorious over his Enemies, in the enjoyment of al ease and plenty, he is stained with the crimes of Adultery and homicide. His son Salomon, floating in a sea of prosperity, became the most unfortunate of men: in a word, our Blessed Saviour confirms this truth by an open declaration, that those are happy who suffer persecution for justice sake : adding, that theirs is the Kingdom of Heaven.

REFLEXION.

Affliction the true badg of a Christian:

THat we might not repine at our condition in this mortal life, which is a warfare upon earth, beset with dangers and hardship; our sweet Redeemer makes use of an argument to his disciples, (and in them to al mankind) unanswerable, and which admits of no reply, saying, I have prepared a Kingdom for you, but tis upon the same terms my father gave it me; I have made this purchase for you at a dear rate, wherefore you must be content to go som little share; but vvithal he hints this comfort, that tho the world should rejoyce, and they be sad, yet their sadnes should be converted into endles joy: nay he adds yet a more charming reason to keep up our spirits in afflictions; the world (says he) wil persecute you because you are mine, so that when we suffer for justice sake, he owns it his quarrel, and wil not fail to render us victorious if with firm footing we stand the brunt but one moment: for indeed the cours of this life is but a moment, nay not so much in respect of Eternity.

With what unwearied labors, and somtimes breaking all the chains of nature and justice, nay endųring the tortures of a guilty conscience, are men carried on to the purchase of an earthly Crown; whilst with patience & quiet submission to Divine Providence, which presides in human affairs, together with the harmony of an innocent interior, we may secure to our selves a Crown Eternal, and which shal never be ravish'd from us. Tis just then that those who stand Candidates for Eternity, should not boggle at the conditions proposed by the Son of God for its acquisition: he was not Crovvnd with glory til the Jews had first placed a Diadem of thorns upon his head: he tasted not the sweets of consolation, before he had tasted gall and vinegar: and why al this? Saint Peter tells us, that we might trace his steps: believing that nothing could have a greater influence to imitation then the prospect of his own actions. Saint Paul assures us that whom God has predestinated, those he moulds to the resemblance of his only son, cloaths them in the same livery, marks them with the same stamp, and gives them the impression of sufferings with his own seal: wherefore I wonder not if the Just be styled by Saint Peter the stones of life, design'd for the structure of the Cœlestial Hierusalem, since they are daily pared with the chizel of adversity, the better to square them for a place in that noble edifice.

Christ our Lord as man, both by word in the Pater Noster, and by example on the Cross, manifested his perfect submission to the wil of his eternal Father, who had decreed he should not enter into his glory but by the way of suffering: why should not we likewise acknowledg an ab-

lute dependance on his sa-
ed dispensations as to our
ncerns in this life? let him
ile or frown upon us we
e sure tis for our good. Our
edience ought to imitate the
ture of faith, which teaches
sublime mysteries are not to
dived in to by the sharpnes
our wit, but with a kind
simple wisdom, Embraced,
lieved, and Adored. So in
lversity, our mind, as relating
Divine providence, ought to
blinded, and no reason
sensd why God does wil, or
rmit us to suffer. Abraham
hen he received that severe
mmand to sacrifice his son,
fled al human, nay Divine

reason which might any wayt put a stop to his obedience, and strugling against the light of reason, and tendernes of a father he proceeds to the Execution of Gods Orders. Wherefore we ought to look upon it as a testimony of our faith when wisely we understand not the mysterious proceedings of providence in our particular concerns: leaving our inordinate wil to be regulated by the unerring direction of the Divine wil. The chief felicity of the Blessed consists in this, that the wil of God is becom their vvil; could vve attain to this conformity, vve should be above malice, or misfortunes:

ties: and as the Philosophers stone turns al it touches into Gold, so should our patience convert al pain into pleasure and al anguish into delights.

How justly then may afflictions be termd the benefits of God since by them we are made the lively images of his son, and by that similitude vve hold our title and claim to his rich Inheritance: vvhy then should vve not set a value on sicknes, loss of our goods, or any other unexpected misfortune, vvhen patience and resignation vvil infallibly open us a passage into heaven?

After this Divine Artist had labour'd to shape us to his ovvn

D.

likenes by fufferings; the next topick he lays hold on to keep us in this form and mould; is in reprefenting to us the little duration vvhich attends our afflictions here : the holy fcripture delineates to us the brevity of this life under feveral Emblems, as of a flovver, a shadovv, a blaft of vvind, and the like; al to fet forth hovv foon it flides avvay : fomtimes involving the shortnes vvith its mifery, tis compared to a vvoman in labor, vvhofe pangs are very fmart, but not lafting: and the pain is mitigated by expectation of a fon : by which is infinuated that the hopes of Beatitude ought to fweeten al the bitternes of adversity.

That great Apostle Saint Paul, who received his commission from heaven to instruct the Gentils, tels them in the first place that the time of this life is short; he adds, that if they be under pressures, they may weep, but so as if they did not weep; that if they had a day of sunshine they might rejoyce, but so as if they only made wrinkles in their face: that they might make use of what goods they found here, but in such a manner as if they were wholly indifferent; and he gives the reason, because there is nothing here we cā call ours: since we are not secure of the poffeffion for on fole moment: confequently vve are not fayd properly to poffes it: vvherefore tis only like a fine Parade, only to be feen in paffing, being always in motion.

Saint Gregory makes a large Panegyric of afflictions, firft in that it compels us to fly unto God, for when our Saviour had foretold his Difciples the fcandals of his Paffion, and how the world would allot the fame meafure to them, he tels them why thefe sharp decrees are made; becaufe (fays he) you should fly to me for fanctuary, and only within my arms feek confolation and security. Again afflictions draw God to us, for he declares by the Royal Prophet he cannot leave the afflicted alone: wherefore you must not think in tribulation, that God is not with you, nor that you are abandoned, if he free you not when you would: for he humors not your wil, but does that which is most expedient for your good.

In fine, Saint Gregory says the just are like to fire wrapt up in a flint, not a spark appears unles forced out by violence: so the vertue of good persons are undiscovered til afflictions make them break forth: tis then their patience, *stian vertues*, I may be thought worthy to appear in your presence, and partake of those ineffable joys reserved for such as suffer here for your name. *Amen.*

THE PROEM. OF SIN.

MY God, after the meditation of your mercyes and benefits, who could imagine (had not dear experience convinced us) there could be such a monster as sin: good turns penetrate the highest mountains, overcom Tygers, yet they work nothing with ungrateful man: give me leave to descant upon this wonder, that finding out the accursed cause which gives birth to sin it may be stifled, and no more destroy infortunate souls.

IV. THAT SIN IS
OPPOSIT TO REASON.

What a horrour to consider how monstrous a thing sin is, that doth evacuate al the designs of God in mans creation! for what contrivance has not our dear Creator set on foot to preserve us in innocence: first imprinting in our natures an innate inclination to felicity; then strengthning this tendency with gracious promises of a Beatitude which comprizes al good imaginable : and left the Charms of happines might not prove sufficiently efficacious to keep us in our duty, he was pleased to add the terrours of the greatest desolation that can enter into our thoughts: but alas man is so unfortunate, as neither the love of happines, nor the fear of misery, can give a stop to bridle his inordinate appetite unto Evil.

REFLEXION.

Sin is a sort of madnes.

ALmighty God designing to make himself our final end, was pleased to prescribe a rule which we are to obferve that we may arrive at this our ultimate Term : this rule is , *to decline what is oppofit to reafon , and by Him prohibited, and perform what is conformable to reafon, and by him enjoynd.* Here we behold the goodnes of God, that having fubjected al the Creatures of this inferior world unto man; him alone, as a noble Creature endued with knowledg and underftanding , he would honor with his commands : and fuch as the prevarication of them feems a myftery hard to be unridled. For in the firft place he forbids nothing but what our reafon goes along with, and judges not fit to be don : nor does he command anything but what our own reason approves, as fit to be put in execution. Hence a sinner at the latter day with great confusion wil find his own reason to rise up, accuse, and play the chief witnes against him, wherefore I wonder not if Saint Basil stile sin a branch of madnes, for is it possible that one in his right wits should wave the courtship of a God omnipotent, who hath fill'd him with blessings here, and reserves more for him in Heaven; to dote with an inordinate affection upon a creature that is a sink of corruption, and has nothing to make him great or happy: to quitt the author of reason and lasting joys for a moments pleasure. Nay, the same Saint affirms that by sin we lose our first understanding which is rational, as if to it succeeded another which favours of a Brutish nature, so he seems to infer that the soul by inordinate acts becomes as it were earthly and fals from the dignity of its creation.

The first effect of sin's frenzy we behold in Lucifer and his adherents; for they knew before their rebellious act, and believed God to be omnipotent, and that any attempt against him would end in their fatal ruin: yet when once they had given consent to what

Pride, and ambition prompted, like furious beasts devoyd of reason they struck at his Throne and Scepter : for which they were banished Heaven, doomd to Eternal flames, and above al, their greatest punishment is, not to be able to stifle their reproaching reason, nor forget the loss of their soveraign good they have incurrd. Thus we see that sin often pushes us on to attempt not only irrational, but even impossible things.

The next sad example we feel in the disobedience of our first Parent Adam, who vested with original justice, endued with knowledg even to perfection, had his choice of al the delights that were in nature; yet his dependence on God ſtuck in his ſtomack, he would be his own maſter, and like unto God: this tickled his fancy, and carried away with a paſſion of Pride, drew upon himſelf and poſterity al the miſeries now incident to mankind.

Thus we ſee the irregular motions of ſin; firſt infringing the laws of God, next the law of our reaſon and ſo deſtroys al that is man in us: for our underſtanding clouded with the darknes of ſin, like one intoxicated with wine, knows he has a habitation, but cannot make one right step to it: so a sinner has a confusd notion of his soveraign good, but overwhelmd with paffion, which is then his guide, he fals into a Labyrinth of vitious acts, which grown into a habit bring him at laft to his inevitable ruin.

To conclude, this diftemper by fin is more eafily prevented then cured, becaufe when once it has taken hold, al the power of nature cannot reftore us to our former condition. Now this foveraign Antidote is Faith actuated and rouz'd up: for we believe a mortal fin deprives us of grace which is the greateft of misfortunes: we
like-

likewise believe that by Gods assisting grace we may becom victorious in any temptation; why then are we not? tis because our faith lyes a sleep, and is as it were dead in us: for did we consider what faith teaches concerning sin, we could not act so contrary to our own reason and eternal interest. Hence the Prophet Ieremy foretold that the earth would be filled with desolation because there is none who look before them, nor weigh the consequence of their actions. Thus an unfortunate sinner, declining the use and dictamens of faith, may justly be styld a Christian only in speculation, but in pra-

E

ctice a meer infidel, nay worſe, for one has the gift and light of faith, whileſt the other alas gropes only in the dusky light of nature.

Nay would men make uſe of their reaſon the very comlines of vertue, and its intereſt would be ſufficient to deter them from vitious actions: for the greateſt part of mankind is influenced and attracted by what is either delightful, glorious, or beneficial; and in al theſe three vertue has the preeminence. If the humor of Ambition ſway in you, what honor ſo great as to be good? it draws veneration even from enemies, that albeit they prosecute their rage as to the exterior, yet they stil retain a value of the person in whom vertue shines. Princes receive not the duty of Obedience, nor Nobles the Ceremonies of respect, but upon supposition of vertue that resides, or ought to reside in them. Are you bewitched with the spel of Avarice? what treasure to be compared to those riches prepared in heaven for the reward of vertues? Riches, not liable to rust, nor to the fear of the hand of rapine. Besides, the competency they enjoy contributes by a moderate use to their health, disturbs not their sleep, and what is unnecessary is employ'd for the relief of the distressed, who are to be witnesses for their claim to eternal felicity. Are you infected with the poison of voluptuousnes? vertue affords satisfaction of the mind, which being more pure and solid then those of the body, does consequently much outstrip them in worth and excellence. O what infatuation then to break the laws of God, our reason, and those of men, (for al human laws ordain punishment for sin) and by these exorbitancies forfeit the honor of vertue unstaind, unfading riches, and pure delights, which are not heel'd with repentance, infamy, nor a cha-

...tisment without end, which ...re the usual consequences of ...nhappy sin.

THE PRAYER.

O God who art an increated wisdom, by whose directing ...ams we ought to steer our actions, ...midst the inconstant waves of this ...oating world: enlighten my un...rstanding with the splendor of ...ur holy spirit, that by its influence ...spersing the clouds of sin, my rea-...n joynd with your grace, may ...eserve me within the limits of ...ur holy commands, and prepare me ...r that crown of justice you have ...omised to those who prove faithful ...e in your service. Amen.

A SINNER IS INJURIOUS TO GOD.

THere is nothing more rational then to acknowledg that Gods supream greatnes exacts a reverence and respect from al creatures, that his infinit goodnes merits al love and fidelity: that his judicial power as being Judg of the living and the dead, ought to beget a fear and trembling in us: yet what a horrour to consider that a sinner denies him al these just rights: setting his laws and commands at naught, and by a strange impudence daring to wrest his scepter from him; for God cannot be God unless he has an absolute command over al creatures; and this prerogative a sinner to his utmost refuses.

REFLEXION.

Sin is a perfect Rebellion.

THere is no crime in a Kingdom or Common wealth so pernicious as that of rebellion; tis like a plague; for from one or two supreamly factious spirits a whole kingdom is set in a flame: just so a sinner disperses his venom thron the whole frame of man, who is within himself a little world: employing the noble endowments of his mind, to wit, his understanding, wil, and memory; which are the great perfections of his immortal soul, to that degree as to mantain a war against his soveraign.

First, whereas the understanding ought to represent unto the wil the happines of our final end, and the lovely shape of vertue, as the delightful means to attain unto it; on the contrary al blinded and overcast with the exhalations of sin, sets before the wil meer illusions and counterfeit objects, which bear the face of som little good, but intrinsically are pernicious, leaving in conclusion nothing behind but a bitter and diftaftful remembrance.

Again, whereas the wil has for its object what is good, nay cannot covet evil under the notion of evil, yet allured, and gaind by the infulting appetite, embraces a creature in defiance of its Creator, loves what it should hate, and hates what it should love, shakes off al depédance on God (to ferve whom is to raign) and exchanges this fweet fervitude to becom a flave to paffions, which fubject man to Avarice, Ambition, Lubricity, and to al the inftruments that malice can frame, to the dishonor of his

Divine Lord and master: for having once induced him to actions below his reason, after this engagement no Tyrany like to this usurper: for he filles the memory with Ideas of sensual pleasures, wherein he is so mired, as nothing appears in him (besides his shape) that is not Brutish: in fine, he employs al his senses to be messengers of his wicked designs, so that the entire composure of a sinner, is an acurate piece of a Rebel, neither awed by majesty, terrifyed by power, nor submissive to authority.

Nay a sinner stops not in his own person, nor by his own faculties to contemn his

Creator, but makes use of the creatures of this inferior world, given him for his service and moderate use, al these he perverts by his inordinate appetite, to the injury of him that gave them; and al this only, to humour a Passion of vanity, Pride, Love, revenge, or som such unlawful motion. In return these creatures as sensible of the il use made of them, wil at the latter day vindicate the honour of their Creator, and the abuse of their being, acted by an ungrateful sinner; every one in its Kind discharging their fury against him.

Lastly, the foulnes of sin appears in that the son of God

employed himself to destroy it; it was for that end he became man, spun out a laborious life of thirty three years to raze it out from the face of the earth: and to reduce man a strayed sheep into the path that leads to his final end, and sovereign good; so that when I sin, it may be truly said, I contemn and trample under foot, the pretious bloud, life, and death of the son of God; and frustrate, as far as lyes in me, the effects of his holy passion. I confes at al times sin appears in a frightful shape, but above al after Christs passion, what can be equal'd to the contempt of his person; of al his sufferings, and to our in-ingratitude for so ineffable a tye and obligation : in this particular reflection of the time, a sinner exceeds the malice of Lucifer, for that struck only at Gods honour as he is a Creator, whereas now we offend God both as he is a Creator, and likewise as he is a Redeemer ; again, Lucifer committed but one sin of Pride, while we daily plunge our selves even in Enormous crimes.

Nay saint Bernard wishes a sinner would contract his malice within the limits of these inferior Creatures, but he becomes so audacious as to attack God in his divine Attributes, wishing he would take no cognizance, at least seem ignorant of his trespasses, by which he would deprive him of his wifdom: or that he would not punish them, and so ravish his Iuftice from him: laftly he wishes he could not chaftife them, and so would render him not Omnipotent.

Besides, the contrariety of God to sin gives a great elucidation to its horror: for God is a fopream Being, sin a nothing, God a source of al beauty, sin a sink of deformity: God is infinitly Iuft, sin is injuftice in the highest degree. O how dreadful a thing is sin, which carries a long with it so many dismal reproaches? But yet much more dreadful when it shal be brought to execution by Divine justice: for to be struck with a million of thunderbolts would appear but like a honydew if compared to the terrour of our angry God, when not restraind by his mercy. Let us then shelter our selves from this desolation by the memory of our last end: let that Memorandum be awake in us and then we shal infallibly pay our God the just tribute of obedience to his holy laws, and consecrate al our endeavours to the promotion of his honor and Glory.

(80)

THE PRAYER.

O God Omnipotent, when I consider your sublimity, and my own abjection, I confes the outrages of sin appear so abominable that were not your mercy infinit, it would be (methinks) presumption even to ask pardon. What a horrour to consider the consequence of sin, for could the effect of what it aims at succeed, it would destroy your Divine life, and in sequel be the destruction of Angels, Men, Heaven, Earth, and al created Beings, who subsist not but by the conserving hand of you their Creator: without whose influence they would in a moment resolve in to

their

their former nothing. Wherefore in the first place I abjure al sin, even to its least exhalation; next I promise never to let this unmerciful monster take birth from my unfortunate wil: and in order to this, I beg that my unhappy soul may be cleans'd in the pretious bloud of the al-immaculate lamb; and by that lotion receiving a dye of innocence, every its motion for the future may contribute to your honour; so that incessantly glorifying you upon earth, I may lay claim to your promises to be glorifyed by you in Heaven. *Amen.*

SIN IS INJURIOUS

To man himself.

Man is framed to the likenes, born to the service, called to the knowledg and enjoyment of a Divinity. To fit him for that great designment God is pleased in Baptism to adorn his soul with grace, a supernatural quality which elevates him above him self; and while we enjoy this pretious gift the son of God owns us for his brethren, and the fruits of his conquest: The Holy Ghost disdains not to make us his temple: nor the

Angels their companions: nay more, al created things here beneath acknowledg man's superiority, so that could this treasure be layd open and here secured to him, he would appear like an earthly God.

REFLEXION.

By sin we forfeit grace, a treasure inestimable.

THere is nothing ought more to amaze us then to consider our partiality in reference to the soul and body: with what solicitude we attend to the one, and how unconcernd in the state of the other: when the body is indispos'd, what care to cal for a Physician, what obedience to his prescriptions: but vvhen the soul is vvounded with sin, how slovv in seeking a remedy, and hovv heedles in avoiding the dangers of a relaps, thô never so home inculcated to us? When the body is in health tis nourisht vvith al delicacies of meat and drink; covered vvith pretious garments, and delighted vvith al sports and pastimes of vanity: vvhile the soul, if so happy as to be in the state of grace, for the most part is fed vvith a cold, tepid devotion, that only keeps her from starving: nay frequently staind vvith venial sins, vvhich take off much of the souls lustre by grace. Novv let us separate, and consider them apart.

As to the body, we know 'tis an earthly piece, a lump of corruption; sorted into several imperfections, insomuch that a main part of our contrivance in this life is taken up in disguising and concealing its defects, that we may be sociable, and entertain our selves in conversation without a blush: whence I wonder not at the saying of a holy person; that Lucifer by the excellence, of his nature was drawn into Pride and thence to his ruine, and to prevent this fatality, Almighty God gave man a body, so to humble him, that while he beheld this object of misery, it might stifle in him Ambition or any other motion of selflove or high conceit: but alas God's design in this proves ineffectual; for the body is most cherisht, and by a strange sottishnes shaped into a meer Idol of vanity.

As to the soul, saint Bernard gives to a holy soul the title of heaven; her understanding (says he) is the sun: her purity and contempt of earthly things, the moon: her vertues, the stars: and her charity the Angel Motor that inspires activity into her actions. Saint Bridgit, who by Gods dispensation was admitted unto a ful view of a soul enricht with grace, assures us, that tis not possible for a mortal eye at once to behold her, and enjoy life, without a particular support from heaven: her beauty would be so ravishing as even to overwhelm a heart with joy: saint Austin styles grace the splendor of a soul, begetting holy love, and consequently a fear to stray from the path of vertue: by the assistance of her rays we arrive to the knowledg of God, our felicity, and the worlds vanity: by the light of this Divine habit, we discover the pleasures of the voluptuous, the wealth of the avaricious, and the dazling glory of the ambitious to be like to a cloud of smoak disperfed into Air, and to contain nothing of solid satisfaction in them. It is grace that displays before us the horror of a mortal sin, and the danger of venial trespasses: it is grace which leads us as it were by the hand into the pleasing observance of God's holy commands: In fine, grace is a participation of the divine nature, and the day-break of that happines the accomplihment of which we expect in heaven: now what a horror to forfeit al these glorious advantages for a moments pleasures:

by one mortal sin we are rendred the vilest of Creatures, declared enemies to God, enslau'd to sathan, odious in the sight of the Angels, and doom'd to suffer endles torments in hel. Wherefore it is more to be lamented then al the disgraces and hardships which can befal us in this world.

Our sweet Redeemer was pleased to honor us with the title of friend, making us the repository (by a friendly communication) of what he had received from his eternal father: now sin makes a breach in al the rules of friendship; it stains us with perfidiousnes towards a God who loved us when with mutinous paſſions in ſcorn of your authority, and in contempt of your higheſt favours: O what infatuation? To believe and acknowledg the ſplendor, and beauty of your fair image within him, and yet proſtitute this treaſure to the deformity of ſin, to ſet up an Idol of vanity, where once you did ſweetly reign in Juſtice and innocence: but while I thus reproach my ſelf, I behold the wonder of your exciting grace, that giving me a ful view of my paſt follies, at the ſame time it gives me an earneſt of your mercy; and is as it were the firſt ſtep to my converſion. For from this reflection I abhor my diſloyalty; I confes I have been treacherous to you and my ſelf; and muſt give *my self lost for ever, unless my tears, groans, and a heart wounded with sorrow and repentance may dispose me for the last stroak of your mercy, and obtain your gracious pardon, which I instantly beg of you the God of mercy. Amen.*

THE PROEM.

Death is the effect of sin, death likewise is the destruction of it: the power of God appears in mans creation, his wisdom in our re-creation: for Christ our Redeemer by the privation of his life restored us unto life; exchanging our temporal into a life eternal: let us admire his love in the myſtery of the incarnation, his juſtice in his paſſion, and bounty in his laſt wil and teſtament in the inſtitution of the ſacred Euchariſt; and after we have entertaind our ſelves with the wonders of his goodnes let us ſpend our ſelves in the praiſe of his mercy.

ON THE MYSTERY OF THE INCARNATION.

OVr unfortunate firſt Parent after his diſobedience was not only exild from paradiſe, that delicious ſeat, and a ſtop put to his celeſtial inheritance, but alſo he involved the maſs of mankind in the punishment: so that his whole posterity groand under the penalty of this sad mortgage: besides his trespas caused so much weaknes in mans nature, such a cloud in his understanding, so much irresolution in his wil, so much disorder in his passions, insomuch that Saint Gregory notes our nature to be so changed as if we were unman'd and becom quite another thing: wherefore we are here to consider, that to restore us to our birthright, to relieve us in this sad plight and desolation, our sweet redeemer took flesh, and became man, in which action appears the testimony of a most rare and incomparable love.

REFLEXION.

Gods love to man.

IF we measure a gift by the dignity of the giver, none can be greater then the instrument of our Redemption; for tis a God that is our benefactor. If by the worth of the gift in it self, tis supreamly valuable, for tis a God that is given: lastly, if by the good wil of the Donor, it admits no dispute, for tis a father that delivers up his son, nay his only son, and whom he infinitly loves, to be our ransom, and to redeem us from the servitude wherein the disobedience

dience of our first Parent had engaged us. This liberality of God seems as it were to blunt the pen of the winged Evangelist, saying; *God so loved the world as he gave unto it his only son.* He expresses with a wonder (*so*) as if he were at a stand, and for the rest left every one to admire what he could not expres: and indeed it may wel cast us into amazement, to behold a God infinit, Eternal, Independent, a soveraign good beatifying the blessed spirits in heaven, to dote upon miserable, ungrateful, and guilty man. That God should cherish the Angels who are immortal spirits, obedient in al things to his laws and wil, who are in the enjoyment of their beatitude, yet infinitly below his greatnes, I say to caress them is no great subject of wonder, but to have a kind regard, nay, a seeming passion of love to man enslaved to vice, unjust, perfidious, and conscious of no Good. O! it surpasses al imagination: but our great and good God designing vve should return to our persecutors good for evil, was pleased to dispose us for this severe command by the exhibition of his holy son as a pledg of Redemption; as also to take away the opprobry of his Creatures. For certainly a sinner is the vilest of Creatures, he is a nothing, that is as to God and his salvation.

It is reported that S. Gregory never beheld the pourtraiture of Abraham with his arm lift up to sacrifice Isaac but it drew tears from his Eyes; and for us to behold the eternal father giving up his dear and only son into the merciles hands of the Jews, and not be sensible of it, is a prodigy beyond al the miracles Christ wrought in his life and passion. Look from the beginning of the world and you wil find a strange series of ingratitude in man: first Adam in a conditon of compleat happines disobedient: Cain a homicide, the rest of his descendents for the most part Idolaters: the Jews, nursed up as it were under his wings, stil rebellious and murmuring, yet stil with an admirable patience supported, nay protected even by miracles: however his goodnes was not restraind, but issued forth his only son to be a Sacrifice for mans redemption. O! how is it possible to sum up al these obligations, and al these testimonies of his love and mercy, and not to becom a perpetual sacrifice of thanksgiving.

Saint Austin hints two very pathetick remarks on Gods munificence in the gift of his only

Son; First in that he has exhausted his divine stock, saying: *O God thô you are Omnipotent, yet you can give no more: thô you are most wise, yet your wisdom can suggest nothing more to give: thô you are the magazine of al treasures, yet tis al emptyed in this profusion of our bounty*: the other remark is, that having made us this present, he can deny us nothing: vvhatsoever vve ask in his name, if to his honour and our good, vvil infallibly be accorded. Nay Saint Chrisostom goes yet further, in extolling the love of God the father, asserting many learned Divines to have declared their opinion that an Angel, or man, might have been raised to such a degree of grace as to be rendred capable of restoring mankind. Novv this suppofition admitted, it transcends al imagination, and argues an exces of love, that his divine majesty should vvave the ministery of his Angels, or the deputation of som man excelling in grace, to engage his son in nature equal to himself, in the severe task of our Redemption: and stil to encrease the wonder, this blessing was showred down upon us, when man had iritated his Creator to that height, that he repented to have made him, that is, were God capable of any error in his actions, this exorbitancy in man might justly merit a repentance.

Since then our sweet Redeemer hath broke throu al these obstacles of our ingratitude, and by a stupendious submission taken our vile nature upon him, what return can we make? certainly we can grudg him nothing: for love consists in a mutual communication of honor, riches, knowledg, and whatever good we posses: now God hath play'd the prodigal with us let us not be penurious to him: he is so reasonable as only to pretend to our heart: *Son* (says he) *give me your heart*; but it must be a heart that is stript of al terrene affection; he is a jealous God and wil have no rival; for in proportion as you love any creature, you have so much the less for him, unless it be in reference to him. There is no greater incentive to love then to prevent a lover; this part God hath acted with us, giving us a pledg of his own dear self; and that heart is very obdurate that wil make no return. O what longing sighs and groans issued from the breasts of those holy Patriarchs in the old law, that they might see the day break of Hierusalem's fair star; with what an awful respect and submission would they have received him: while we with a kind of stupidity gather the fruit of his divine influence, without lifting up our eyes, or paying the least acknowledgment to him from whence they flow.

Saint Thomas says that the Benignity of God appears very great in that he daigns to communicate himself to the just by grace, but much more daigning to cõmunicate himself in the unity of his person to the human nature of IESUS CHRIST. the Prophet Osee ch. 11. foretold this mystery of love: saying, that God would link us to him by the chains of Adam, that is, God-man; for beholding the affections of men drawn by visible objects to that as ever to be induced to Idolatry, his love prompted to render him self visible by taking flesh, so to humour our inclinations, and becom an object to which we may justly pay the honour of Latria, or Divine worship: thus love contrived that his sacred humanity should serve as a bait by which they might be allured to place their Adorations aright. In this mystery the seal is set to declare the worlds perfection; for by it we receive the remission of our sins, sanctifying grace and eternal glory: faith, exciting grace, and al the motions to our salvation are the effects of this sacred mystery. To conclude, by it the honour of God is repared, his service advanced, his creatures put into a vvay of safety, and his enemies confounded. Let us therefore seriously weigh the benefits of Christ Incarnation, that from thence we may cherish our hopes to praise and glorify God for the exhibition of so inestimable a gift for the reparation of mankind.

THE PRAYER.

MY sweet Redeemer, who art a true sun of justice, sent to make an attonement between your Eternal father and the perisht world: and in sequel

(108)

to clear for us a passage unto heaven: enlighten us with your beams of mercy, that by vertue of this reconciliation we may here be freed from al stains of sin, and in the other life be restored to our lost inheritance, which we shal ever ow to you O Incarnate Word. Amen.

VI. A MEDITATION ON THE PASSION.

The August Mystery of Christs passion merits rather to be celebrated with silence and wonder then with tongue, or pen; its sublimity surpasses the capacity of Angels, that God should dye for man;

a master for his slave, a Creator for his creature, and an innocent for the guilty: whence Saint Basil tearms the Passion a perpetual mystery; because it reaches to the salvation of al men: so that this Sacrament of reconciliation wil never cease while the world endures; therefore may justly be ascrib'd to the supream goodnes of Gods special love in redeeming, not Angels, but men; not by another, but by himself: not by an unbloudy, but the bloudy death of the Cross. Saint Bonaventure makes it an argument of his special love to man, in that he gave up his life, not for Angels, but for man; and the world for mans sake; believing that an Angel was deputed to give a constant motion to the Cœlestial bodies: for he look'd upon Angels far surpassing men in excellence, and by consequence not so fit for his supream wisdom to render them so serviceable to him. Now what judgment would he have passed upon our Christian belief, that teaches not only the world to be framed for our use, but also the Creator himself to becom man, nay even to stoop to nothing, that man might be partaker of his Divine nature. Wherefore by how much the lower he threw himself, so much the more he ought to be be raised in our affection : by how much the greater was our misery, so much the more our obligation is increased to our Saviour who freed us : and as his humiliation had no measure, our gratitude in like manner ought to go along in the same proportion.

The characters of Gods love are drawn out in such plain colours, that none can be so stupid as to plead ignorance; they are writ in bloud, and the Prophet in the person of Christ invites us to cast our eyes upon them ; saying : al you that pass by the way make a stand , consider my present condition, and tel me if there be any grief like unto mine. At the firſt entrance into this tragedy ſaint Paul (Hebr. 12.) tels us that Chriſt had a pleaſant ſcene propoſed unto him : that is, glory, or ignominy, a Regal appearance here an earth, or a ſervile condition, the redemption of mankind, either by way of cruelty or meeknes, was given to his election : for one groan from his heart, one tear from his pretious eye, or one drop of his bloud, had been ſufficient to have redeemd millions of worlds, yet that he might convince us of his exceſſive love, and apply a plenitude of remedies, ſo to draw us to acts of gratitude, and to pitty ourselves, he rather chose the Cross; he emptied his sacred veins, afflicted his soul with anguish and sadnes; permitted his body to be torn with stripes, insomuch that from al the parts of his body, the bloud streamd out; whence saint Bernard gives an ingenious remark: that albeit nature afforded him but two eyes, to be the conduits of tears, yet every pore of his body supplied his visive power, issuing forth a floud of crimson sweat, the most prodigious effect of anguish that ever happened in nature: to the end that with them, as with tears, he might expiate our faults, and wash away the ordures of sin. Saint Chryfoſtom hints another reaſon of this his ſeverity to himſelf, that he might hamper us in the Chains of his love; for there is nothing enſlaves a perſon like to a good turn, or obliging act of friendſhip: wherefore Saint Bonaventure aſſerts, that nothing could have faſtned the ſon of God to the Pillar but a link of Charity.

In the revelations of ſaint Bridgit, examined by order of the Council of Baſil, and declared as iſſuing from a ſpirit Divine, to which we might rationally give credit, 'tis related, that the extremity of

Chrifts dolorous paffion, rent his heart afunder, and open'd him a paffage unto death; for certainly no expiring perfon was ever fo deftitute of comfort as our fvveet Redeemer. The reafon is, his foul applying it felf to the vifion of the Divine effence, left the fentitive parts al defolate, hence vvas iffued forth that difmal cry that God had forfaken him, for whereas a good perfon fuffering in a juft caufe ufualy cheers himfelf with the confideration of the brevity of his fufferings, the reward he expects in recompence, and the like, al this our Bleffed Saviour waved, wholly intent on the contemplation of the beatifick vision; so that the Prophet Esay had just reason to style him a man of grief, and dolours. 'Tis true twas in his power not to dye, wherefore he frankly gave up his life, and since he had undertaken the redemption of mankind, he would compleatly satisfie the Divine justice, suffering in his body to the utmost that rage could throw upon him, withdrawing likewise his intellectual faculties from lending any succour or spark of consolation to his sensitive parts, to that degree as even to shiver his heart in pieces, O what a prodigious testimony of love.

If every wound of Lazarus

was as so many tongues to move the rich man to compassion, how loud ought Chrifts paffion to found in our ears, and Court us unto gratitude, to behold him naild to the Crofs, so cruelly fcourged that his whole body appear'd but as one woūd, crownd with thorns, befmeard with fpittle, laden with iniuries, at laft expiring on the Crofs, and al this for our fake: O it is impoffible ferioufly to confider al this, and our hearts not diffolue into love and compaffion. Our divine Redeemer feems to fay that the utmoft teftimony of love is to lay down ones life for a frend, but methinks hifelf did much more when he did it for his Enemies. Man sets not his affection upon any thing, unless it appear fair, wise, pleasant, pretious, or good: now God beheld nothing attractive in us; we were odious, vile, perfidious, and miserable; yet out of his goodnes he would purify and cleans us in his own bloud, he communicates favours to the ungrateful, to render them grateful; to his enemies, to make them friends, and to the distressed that he may render them happy, purchasing for them by his death immortality. How justly then may we conclude that the accomplishment of Gods love to man is evident and compleated in his Passion.

THE PRAYER.

MY sweet Redeemer, when I contemplate your suffering posture on the Cross, methinks I should becom a statue with admiration and wonder: could my eyes distil a deluge of tears, and my heart with sorrow shiver into pieces, yet my compassion ought not there to rest: had I as many lives as there are grains of sand in the Ocean, and al consecrated to your honour, yet would they not reach to the least degree of compensation for that pretious life of yours, of which one moment is more valuable then al the duration of Angels: what return then shal I make? At last I per-

ceive tis love alone and gratitude you expect; wherefore I wish, my dear Redeemer, that my heart were a furnace heated with the flames of seraphins, that I might be a perpetual sacrifice of love, praise and thanksgiving for your immense favours in the sacred mystery of your passion. Amen.

VII. ON THE INSTITUTION OF THE EUCHARIST.

This Epitome of wonders, the sacred Eucharist, may justly be termed an extension of Christs love in his Passion: for Christ offered up himself once only a bloudy sacrifice on mount Calvary: but in the

Eucharist he is dayly offered up an unbloudy sacrifice in millions of places, by which the memory of his passion is renew'd, and the fruit thereof applyd. In mans creation God breath'd into him a life obnoxious unto death. In the Eucharist he communicates unto him a supernatural and immortal life. In mans creation, corporeal creatures were rank'd under his subjection: in the Eucharist, the Creator of heaven and earth is given up to his command. In the incarnation Christ took upon him the form of a slave, in the Eucharist he shrowds himself under the species of bread and wine, which being accidents are much more despicable then a human form, nay I dare say, it is not only an extension of love in his Passion, but even it exceeds it: for God more hates the guilt of sin then its punishment; consequently, to be crown'd with thorns, and naild to the Cross, was to him more supportable, then to be toucht by sacrilegious hands, applyed to a prophane mouth, and harboured in an impious breast: for the punishment of sin is not unworthy a God, yet the malice of it is opposit to his Divine nature.

REFLEXION.

Gods love and Passion perpetuated.

HOly writers affirm that al the torments Christ suffered in the whole scene of his Passion, were not so afflictive as the presence of Judas a domestick, an Apostle and a Traytor: it is a greater argument of perfection, to love an enemy then a friend: after death Gods faithful servants are beatified in heaven, his enemies doomd to perpetual punishment in hel: now tis not so in the Eucharist; he excludes none from his table, tho innocent and guilty are admitted to that heavenly banquet: a Iudas partakes of his body together with his beloved Disciple; it is born to a thatch'd house as readily as to the Pallace of a King, to shew that in this institution of the Blessed Sacrament, Chrifts love to mankind is not only perpetuated, but compleated even to its utmost perfection.

It is usual at the parting of friends for the spirits to fal into commotion, and send forth most tender expressions: this evidences the great affection God had for man, that being to return to his Eternal father he contrived a means to be always with us, I say such a contrivance that nothing but love could have found out : a contrivance that sets out his love even beyond our Creation, or redemption. O what a Prodigy of love, that while his enemies were framing a crown of thorns for him, at the same time he gave a Pledg to us for a crown of glory : that while they designd him to the highest infamy, he opens them a way to supream felicity. This made the Evangelist inculcate that he loved us to the last : tis now at his departure that he musters up al his forces, to shew what love can do, and indeed tis such an effect as none but a love Divine could produce and therefore of al the Sacraments it is styled the most perfect. Not only Gods inefable love, but likewise his Omnipotence shines in this August Sacrament: what a cluster of miracles are heaped one upon another? first nature is turnd topsy turvy, bread and wine as it were annihilated, or reduced to nothing by words of the priest: the species or accidents deprived of their subject, yet subsisting like clouds in the air without any support, and serving as a vail to shroud under them the glorious majesty of God, to be in millions of places at the same time: his entire body contracted within the

the compas of a little host, and al these wonders to be acted daily to the worlds end. Now the drift of al this is that the fruit of his Passion might always be applyd to us; and that the belief of his real presence might strike an awful respect and reverence into us; together with astonishment that his infinit majesty should stoop so low as to be united to the lovvest of created things, that is, the species of bread and vvine: another motive is, that since by the work of our Redemption, Christ had only given life to our souls, by the purchase of grace, leaving our bodies under the penalties caused by Original sin, until their glorification at the general resurrection; wherefore to compensate this delay, and supply the prerogatives of Original justice, he was pleased to afford us his own glorious and immortal body, which raises us to a life of grace, a life eternal, over which death has no power: Christ asserts it, saying, He that eats of this bread shall live for ever. while he conversd among men he exhibited his sacred person to be the object of our sight and Adoration, but in the Eucharist he intimately unites himself unto us and makes us one with him: for as material nourishment gives a certain temper to the body corresponding to its nature, so this bread of Angels (if worthily received, and with al due circumstances) imprints in the soul the very qualities, Inclinations, and vertues of JESUS CHRIST: nay enriches her with the merits of his holy Passion.

Now that we may arrive at this perfect union, let us do the utmost of our endeavours, divest and clear ourselves of every the least imperfection, that this heavenly Guest may find nothing to hinder the effects of this his divine presence, when we approach to that heavenly table.

Which effects are, first to transform and incorporate himself into us.

Secondly, to cast into our breast som sparks of that inflamd love, wherewith he designd to set the world on fire, declaring he came for that end, that it might consume al things here beneath.

Thirdly, to give me a previous relish of heavenly delights, and at the same time cause in me a distast of al that's visible here on earth.

Lastly, to enlighten me with a certain knowledg of what the divine wil and pleasure is, and in sequel, to communicate his grace, and powerful aid to put it in execution.

Now while I contemplate the wonders of a holy communion, I confes I am no less seized with admiration, that after so many communions, I am stil a stranger to these so admirable effects. But again I am satisfied when I reflect that tho by receiving this Blessed Sacrament, unstaind with any mortal sin, I am enriched with the principal effect which is sanctifying grace; yet as to the forementiond prodigious effects there are required many necessary conditions.

First, a great purity of conscience, together with a renouncing of al worldly vanity or interests.

Next, to have no adhesion, or complacence even in any venial sin.

Lastly, to be in perfect charity with the whole world. Let us therefore endeavour to fit ourselves with these requisites that we may be so happy as to be blessed in the participation of the divine liberality exhibited in the ever adorable Sacrament of the holy Eucharist.

THE PRAYER.

O God, the fountain of al goodnes, who invites the thirsty unto streams which for ever wil allay their drougth; and likewise courts the weary unto a repast, where they shal be nourished with the food of Angels: give me I beseech you a distast of al other refreshments, and fit me with a nuptial garment by which I may be rendered a pleasing guest to you the Bridegroom, who hast promised to Espouse such as are so vested, by an eternal Alliance in the bonds of love and mercy. Amen.

Remember thy last end, and thou shalt never sin. Eccl.7.40.

THE PROEM.

THe final end of man, composed of soul and body, is distinguisht into that of a mortal life, which is death, and into a life immortal which is felicity, or infelicity: that is, to be eternaly happy, or eternaly miserable; for there in no mean, one of these extreams must infallibly be his lot or doom.

VIII. A MEDITATION UPON DEATH.

When I consider death with the train of corruption, stench, and a hideous deformity which attends and follovvs it, I confes it strikes me into horrour and admiration. First what a horrour to consider a body, kept with al nicety, preserved with al rarities, no cost, art, or industry, wanting to render it fresh, and lively, in a moment to becom a lump, liveles, ugly, noisom, and after a while made a prey to worms: witnes the fair Elizabeth, Empres to Charles the fifth, the wonder of beauty in her time, soon after death became so deform'd, and such a stench issued from her, as it occasion'd the Duke of Gandia, then present, to bid adieu to al the worlds vanities, and shrovvd himself within the wals of a holy Cloister.

✠

REFLEXION.

How beneficial the thoughts of Death.

AH! did we as oft behold ourselves in a deaths head (which wil be one day the true image of us) as now we do in a glafs, so many precious hours would not be thrown away in adjusting a lock of hair, a patch, or knot of riband, so much art and so many inventions would not be contrived, to set out and preserve a beauty, that with every little indisposition, or malecontented humour is altered and impaird; nay liable to a thousand accidents for its total ruine. The same consideration would also teach men to change their adorations into a blush, and reserve their passions for a beauty unfading: that beauty (says Saint Austin) alone merits that name, which as it is fair and lovely, continually remains so: a beauty that knows no setting sun, but is always vested with a meridian glory. Let us therefore learn of the Royal Prophet this prudent lesson, to remember our last end, to remember we must dye, and be resolued into dust. If our days pass away like a shadow, no less does beauty like a flower; fair in the morning, and at night drooping in its withered leaves. Besides if we re-

(140)

Act, that the most charming beauty hath oft proved very fatal both to the owner and lookeron, this reflection ought to check any appetite or desire of appearing so accomplish'd; especialy since it may contribute both to their own and others ruine. In a word, remember, that the glory, pomp, riches, and esteemd happines of this world, descend not with us to the grave, al we bear from hence is our good and bad deeds.

THE PRAYER.

O God, who in the noble structure of man hast allotted

him a soul immortal that resembles
your Divine Being, with power to
command his inferior and sensitive part; enlighten me to know
the dignity of my spiritual substance,
and in conformity to what you have
ordain'd, grant that I may render
this earthly piece of mine, that is
my body, instrumental to acts of
Piety, and what I ow to you my
Creator; that since I am in-
trusted with it to make it happy
for eternity, I may keep it in subjection, treat it as my slave, absolutely depending on me, and never
acquiesce to its fawning and en-
chanting alluremnets, lest I contribute to the eternal ruine of both.
Amen.

flect, that the most charming beauty hath oft proved very fatal both to the owner and looker on, this reflection ought to check any appetite or desire of appearing so accomplish'd, especialy since it may contribute both to their own and others ruine. In a word, remember, that the glory, pomp, riches, and esteemd happines of this world, descend not with us to the grave, al we bear from hence is our good and bad deeds.

THE PRAYER.

O God, who in the noble structure of man hast allotted

him a soul immortal that resembles
your Divine Being, with power to
command his inferior and sensitive part; enlighten me to know
the dignity of my spiritual substance,
and in conformity to what you have
ordain'd, grant that I may render
this earthly piece of mine, that is
my body, instrumental to acts of
Piety, and what I ow to you my
Creator; that since I am in-
trusted with it to make it happy
for eternity, I may keep it in subjection, treat it as my slave, absolutely depending on me, and never
acquiesce to its fawning and en-
chanting allurements, lest I contribute to the eternal ruine of both.
Amen.

VIII. THE SECOND MEDITATION

OF DEATH.

What a horrour to consider that the sacred bonds of mariage, the strictest tyes of nature and friendship, al dissolued in death; no chains of Alliance, or worldly interest of proof against his destructive hands: no Presidens having yet been found to flatter us with the least hopes of escaping his icy paws, no condition of eminent dignity, neither youth, beauty, eloquence, or treasures could ever yet corrupt, or blunt his unmerciful sithe which mows down al before him.

REFLEXION.
The certainty of death.

Since then the decree of death is past, and is more inviolable then that of the Medes and Persians: let us at least solace ourselves with this, that death in its self is indifferent; to those that dye in grace it is good, to those that die in sin it is evil: wherefore you see it is in our power to render that thing so terrible quite of another nature; as the Psalmist says: the death of saints is pretious in the sight of God.

THE PRAYER.

O God in whose hands are lodg'd the Keys of life and death, and who hast put me into this world (moved thereunto by your goodnes) without any desert, or knowledg of mine: grant that whilst I wander in this foreign Region far from my home, I may learn and punctualy observe a lesson, short, but comprehensive, issuing from your own blessed mouth, which is; To love you above al things, and my neibour as my self. The performance of the one wil carry me quietly to my grave, freeing me from any act of injustice or satisfaction to render at my death: while the

other

other wil cast me into languishments after you the object of my love, stil awaiting that sleep which may convey me throu the ecclips of death, into the splendor of a life eternal, and into the accomplishment of al my hopes and desires. Amen.

THE THIRD MEDITATION

OF DEATH.

What a horror to behold a person who has placed his felicity in the goods of this world, forced to surrender up al at the approach of death, and this perhaps at a time when little prepared for acts of Iustice; or when in the height of contentment in pofseffion of som pleafing object; no tears or terrours, no groans or importunities can obtain any refpit; when he fummons, we muft go; for death has no eyes to be dazled at the fplendor and majefty of great ones; nor ears to be moved with the howlings of the miferable: Ah what pleafure then can it be to enjoy that which in a moment may be fnatch'd from us, or we from it. The day of our Lord which is death fteals upon us like a theif in the night: befides we are wholly ignorant both of the manner, and what kind of death shal conclude our life, as also of the place, or time.

REFLEXION.

Thoughts of death prevent illusions.

Whilest in health we are cheated by disguises, and false appearances of things, but at the lightning of death every thing is represented in its right proportion. A dying person wil tel you that al his past sensual delights appear to him like a dream, and he wishes they had been so: for then he should awake with joy to sleep again in death, with hopes of enjoying pure and lasting pleasures: he wil tel you that honour, greatnes and esteem of men are a meer shadow, a puff of wind, or a little smoke, which like a vapour vanish at the Evening of our life: he wil tel you that his inordinate appetite in the purchase of a fortune, his continual fears to be disturbed in the possession, and his ambition to make a figure in the world, have diverted him from the pursuit of never perishing treasures, which ought to have been the sum of his endeavours here upon earth. Learn therefore in time this lesson issuing from an expiring breath, which is of weight because esteemd most sincere. For at last it wil be too late to be undeceived: look I say betimes into the glass of death, you may there learn both to live and dye: for death not only teaches, but forewarns and povverfully perſvvades.

THE PRAYER.

1. *Adore your providence, my God, that to the short period of this our life, you have added a draught of gal to be mingled with the sweets of this world; that since really we are pilgrims, we ought not to fix our contentment in any pleaſing object here, but ſtil advance on our way towards the manſion of our eternal repoſe: May I then O my God be ſo happy as to make uſe of thoſe creatures your liberal hands*

have bestow'd, according to the tenour of their Grant, which is to be aiding to me in works of your service: give me an aversion for riches, unles I use them so as to encrease my treasures in heaven; let me contemn honour and greatnes, if in the least they divert me from obedience to your laws: In a word, let me set a value upon every thing in proportion as is may contribute to your honour and glory, and to the security of my souls eternal interest. Amen.

THE FOURTH MEDITATION

OF DEATH.

WHat a horror to consider the separation, and sad

parting of soul and body, after a long union and friendship, imprinted by God and nature in them: the one to be resolu'd into dust, whilst the other is hurried to a Tribunal before an impartial Judg, there to answer for every idle word or thought: and al-uncertain of her doom, whether to be rejoyn'd in a state of happines or misery, and this for no less than Eternity.

REFLECTION.

Thoughts of death the best armour against the day of judgment.

A Christian taught by faith that there is a judgment

to enfue upon the feparation of foul and body, ought not to live as if he vvere immortal, or as if he had no account to render at the latter day, but carefully to provide againſt the time of that dreadful Aſſiſe, where vvil be ſcan'd to the ful and vvith the ſevereſt ſcrutiny al our good and bad actions, in order to an eternal revvard or punishment: and this trial appears the more terrible in that al our trefpaſses directly ſtrike againſt the honour of him vvho is to be our Iudg. For Chriſt having pay'd our ranſom by the effuſion of his pretious bloud, has this prerogative decreed him to be both

Iudg and Party. O what a confusion for a sinner to behold his offended Iudg, who was once to him a patient God, and whom then he contemnd, disobeying his just laws: who was once to him a loving God, and whom then he slighted, more valuing a petty interest of this world, or som foul momentary pleasure, beyond al the endearments and testimonies of his real affection. What a confusion to hear a particular list given in and publish'd, of al those graces and favours he had received from the liberal hands of his once indulgent father, and now his sovereign Iudg; as also a clear recital made of al his ungrateful returns, in sequel, this a merciful lamb, then becom a Lion, vvil let loose al the reserve of his anger to fal upon his guilty head. The first effect vvil be to brand him vvith the black stamp of the highest ingratitude, vvhich mark of eternal shame, one would think, to a generous soul would be a sufficient punishment, without the addition of those horrid torments ordaind by Divine justice to be inflicted on perisht souls. Now to dispose ourselves for a happy issue in this grand proces the best expedient is to retain a constant memory of death; for death not only minds us that it is a privation of life, an up shot to al our pleasures here, the lofs of al our goods and poffeffions, in a word a casheering of al our earthly defigns, but it alfo lays open before us our entrance into another life, and the hazardous gulf we are to pafs throu ere we com to be happy: the way then to fecure our happines is frequently to lodg our thoughts in a fepulcher, and this as is at hand, and rapping at our door. For fuch perfons (fays Saint Auftin) wil be like ftars, not feen in the day of this life, but glitter and fparkle in the night of Death.

THE PRAYER.

MY God, there is nothing more dreadful then your abused love converted into hatred, and to a love injured usually succeeds the like measure of punishment; what terrour then, my God, wil invade a sinner, at the latter day when al the mysteries of divine love to mankind shal be lay'd open: the sacred wounds my Redeemer receiu'd upon our score, and which then shal outstrip the sun in brightnes, wil sufficiently evidence your excessive love, and our extream ingratitude. Those sacred scars I say, wil also justify your fury issuing from an irritated love, *whilst our apparent guiltines wil find no plea, no retreat to shelter it self from your consuming anger: O my God, grant that I may in time foresee this helples desolation, and prepare against it; the time of this life is the time wherein the flouds of your mercy are drawn up; O let me be so happy as now to bath my self in those purifying streams; and may I by acts of love and repentance, purchase here a quiet submission to death, and at the ensuing judgment a joyful invitation to take my place at your right hand. Amen.*

THE FIFTH MEDITATION
OF DEATH.

COnsider the goodnes of God that notwithstanding man would not be forewarn'd of Death, yet he has ordain'd in his wisdom to make it a warning piece against sin: to this end he decreed that the hour of its approach should be wholly uncertain, and lye hid unto us; by that means to strike us into a fear of surprisal, and render us very wary in the conduct of our life, lest being snapt unawares, the ballance of our good actions may prove to light at the grand accounting day. Wherefore Christ taught us in our Pater noster to supplicate for our daily bread, because he never promis'd us a to morrow. Besides, death looks upon at a great distance squares not our life to any Rule of prudence, it neither diverts from what is evil, nor allures to what is good: but to those who make it the subject of their daily meditation and daily expectation, its arrival can do no harm.

REFLEXION.

Thoughts of death prevent surprisals.

IN the first place such persons wil have no remors of conscience, having made their life a preparation to death: next, they wil have no reluctance to quit their possessions here, because they look'd upon them only as goods instrusted, or lent, and to be restored at the owners demand: hence they having not set their heart upon them, chearfully they make a surrender and with smiles approach to grim death, carried on with hopes to make it a passage to the enjoyment of Paradise, the sweet air of eternal mansion seeming already to affect their nostrils, and prompt them to invite this pale ferry-man to waft them over; for tho the glory of the world descend not with sinners, yet the glory of vertue descends with the just.

THE PRAYER.

O God who hast given man a restless appetite after his sovereign good, and hast decreed that death must usher him to this his happiness, there being nothing here beneath to quiet his unsatisfied desires; we bless your immense goodnes in rendring our abode in this vale of tears so fleeting, as also the hour of our last sleep so uncertain, that we may neither be too long detaind from the enjoyment of our glorious final end, nor unprepared at that summons which shal call us from the tumultuous Ocean of this world unto the haven of eternal rest, which throu your mercy we hope the constant thoughts of death may secure us. Amen.

FURTHER REFLEXIONS UPON DEATH.

AFter these dismal considerations, I am likewise cast into wonder and amazement; in that we sport, and play, caress and recreate our selves, even when we are dying, and perceive it not. Gods threathing words to Adam make it evident, saying, *on the very day he eat of the forbidden fruit, he should dye.* Now Adam lived many years after: the meaning therefore is, at the very moment of his transgression he should begin to dye; hence Saint Gregory terms our life a lingring death, for the first motion of our life is likewise a motion unto death, every succeeding hour, month, or year, is the death of the former never again to return: so that we pass (as it were) from one grave to another, til at last we com to our winding-sheet, which only is called death, because the last change, or vicissitude of life, thô a great part of us were dead before, albeit we were not sensible of it, so that in reality we are a living sepulcher to ourselves. How justly then may our life be term'd death, since it is in a perpetual motion, and chang, never fix'd by any stability; but always in a rapid cours. hurried on towards its end. Now, at the first glance of mans sad condition under the fatality of death, I confess my repining thoughts are alarmd; but no sooner I reflect on the sweet proceeding of our Creator in this particular, when al murmuring is changed into admiring his incomparable goodnes. For God creating our first Parent placed him in the most delicious climate of the habitable world, adornd him with original justice, which made a fine harmony throu out the whole frame of man: his inferior part, and senfitive appetite, perfectly obedient, and submissive to his reason: no storms of passions or irregular motions prompting him to evil; now that he might not fal from this happines, God was pleas'd to terrify him with the confequence of his tranfgreffion, which should be death, as a punishment more affrighting than that of hel; for death is obvious to our reafon and fenfe: reafon tels us that a compound of feveral elements naturally refolves into thofe principles whereof it is compofed: our fenfes likewife daily behold the havock made in mankind by death: now that there is a hel Faith only gives us the knowledg; and how unactive this vertue is in any vehement temptation we need go no further to convince us then our own fad experience; hence tis evident death fprings from fin, for had there been no difobedience, there had been no death, Adam's sottish incredulity not believing he should dye, drew death upon his own head, and al his posterity. Next, tis clear, the wisdom of God (to our apprehension) could not contrive a greater Bugbear then the terrour of death avoid sin, nor consequently a more powerfull expedient to secure immortality to us.

My God I adore your ineffable goodnes that vvas pleas'd to put immortality into our hands vvhich our first parent might easily have grasp'd, and secur'd to himself and posterity.

I adore no less your mercy, that when we had forfeited this pregious gift of immortality, you did not at the same time deprive us of your dear self, as our final end, and sovereign good, tho throu our own fault we were to pass to it by death; nay more, to render the purchase of our final end less hazardous, was pleas'd to ordain the time and hour of our death to be wholly uncertain, lest sinners might persever in their wickednes with hopes of som respit for repentance; or the just slacken their devotions, reserving the more fervent acts of vertue towards the end of their life. God (says S. Austin) wrapt up in secret the last day of our life, that we should observe every day as if it were our last. Let us keep close to this rule;

then death (which is now so terrible) wil put an end to our pilgrimage here, be the upshot of our misery, a return from our banishment, and an entrance into our eternal happines.

Wherefore my God from this present I submit to the sentence of mortality you have pronounced against me, and this I do, not by constraint, or to obey the necessity of nature, but meerly in that it is a decree of your Divine wil, to which I comform my self: as also to that manner of death you have determind as to my particular, and to it's circustances without any exception.

From this present I resign my self to that last sicknes which shal give a period to my life, unproferably trifled away; and I offer up my agony in union of those dolorous pangs my dear Redeemer suftaind upon the Crofs.

I reprefent to my felf the horrour my diffigured body may give to others which I accept of as a punifhment for my felflove and efteem of others. I alfo refign to be caft into oblivion after my death, as a juft return, for having been fo little mindful of you my God during my wretched life.

Laftly, I fubmit to my bodies corruption in my grave, in expiation of al my pamperings, and inordinate pleafing of my appetite: and likewife in fatisfaction for that large fcore I ow to your Divine Majefty for my coldnes and tepidity in your service.

THE PROEM.

After this great work of our Redemption, by whose vertue the gates of geaven are layd open, let us convert our thoughts and desires towards that celestial abode; where no more the ugly shape of sin, nor terrours of death shal affright: where no more the fear of our own frailties shal keep us in an awful trembling, being confirmd in grace: and where al our toilsom labours upon the score of vertue wil be converted into eternal rest: wherefore this shal be the subject of our next meditation and the conclusion of al: for having brought you thither, no more remains but to love and praife for eternity.

IX. THE DIGNITY OF MANS'S FINAL END.

When God created al things of nothing he alone was exiftent, what then could he have in his eye but him felf to be the final end of al his vvorks? vvherefore to the inferior Creatures in this vvorld he is their final end, but to Angels and Men vvho are endued vvith reafon, he is not only their final end, but alfo their objective Beatitude. Hence appears the excellence of human nature vvhich is equaly rank'd vvith Angels: for the value of every being is derived from the end to vvhich it is defigned : novv the end of man being the fame vvith that of the bleffed fpirits, confequently he is not inferior to them in the high prerogative of his Being. That he is our final end, Saint Auftin fvveetly infinuates, faying: *My God, should you give me al you have made, yet vvithout your felf they would not reach to quiet my inclination which cannot be centerd but in you alone.* And that he is our objective beatitude, or fovereign good, this affurance Almighty God imparted to Abraham, declaring, *that he himself would be our too great reward.* That is too great for our merit, tho not for his love.

REFLEXION.

Means to attain unto our final end.

THere is nothing more delightful then to contemplate God's method in the framing, and Compleating man from his creation to his consummation. First he was pleased to draw him out of nothing, and give him a simple natural Being, yet a Being so far surpassing in excellence all other Creatures of this inferiour world as it justly prefigured som rare design of this great Artist.

Next, Almighty God beholding this his work immediately depraved by sin, and throu man's own fault ungrateful to him that made him, yet he would not let him perish, but as at first he had dragd him from nothing by his pure goodnefs, fo likewife he would referve him by a greater teftimony of his goodnes from the evil Being of fin, which is wors then nothing as Chrift declared of his treacherous Apoftle, *it were better he had never been*. And to effect this he defignd, that wonder of love, and mercy in the miftery of our Redemption.

Laftly our great, and good God whofe bountyes are beyond meafure and incomprehenfible was fo carryed on by his paternal affection to man, as his gift of natural Being by Creation, and that of grace by Redemption did not fil up the extent of his liberality, for he beheld them intermingled with the miseryes of this mortal life, wherefore he daigned to superad the excellent Being of glory; by the communication of his divine essence by an ardent love, a perpetual joy, and by a profusion of al accessaries which attend so sublime, and supereminent a state of bliss.

Now to have the charming sweetnes of our final end deciphered to us, and yet remain ignorant of the means by which we may, arrive unto it, would affoard us very little satisfaction, know therefore we are to cut out our way to this blessed state by vertuous, and pious actions; t'is true God might have given it without exacting any thing

at our hands, but the order of his Providence hath decreed, that with labour and pain, we should attain to our utmost perfection: nor ought we to repine that so great a good should cost us a little sweat, and hardship; especially if we reflect how unweariedly we toyl our selves in the pursuit of fading treasures besides, God assists us with his grace, and supernatural ayds, which joynd whith the knotty, combats a virtuous man sustains do proportion his good works to the greatness of beatitude, do purify, and prepare him for that sublime state. Whence Philo terms Industry the supereminent treasure of man and in sequel adds that
no-

nothing great or generous is to be expected from a person who gives himself to ease and pleasure. For God did not Create man, and enrich him with so many different habits, and facultyes, that he should keep his arms across and do nothing; man's ful repose is not like that of a stone which arriu'd at its center is unmoued, and without action: but as here we are to be industrious, so in the term a soul is not reputed happy but when actually in the enjoyment of God, tasting his sweetness, and intimately uniting her self to his essence, from whence, as from a breast she sucks a deliciousness that surpasses all imagination wherefore to dispose man for the purchase of this his utmost perfection.

He hath an appetite concreated with him, by which he naturally loves God, and moves towards him as to his Center; besides this motion inserted in his nature, he is endued with another appetite, which is a liberty granted to act without any constraint; so that'tis in his power to pursue this or that object at his choice, and tis from the management of this appetite, or free will, he becomes happy or miserable. Now this noble faculty is well directed when it moves, and is united to the will of God according to his precept: for then God by his povver enables him to act; by his vvifdom regulates his actions; and by his goodnes applies them to himfelf as their final end. Then this free vvil happily addreffed renders mans vocation fecure, by flight from fin and the practice of vertue.

But again, vvhen this free vvil is il addreffed by deviating from Gods commands, acting both againft reafon and obedience; God immediately ftops his activity, lends him no more his directing beams, for his goodnes cannot cooperate to vvhat is evil; hence unfortunate man quitting his al guiding fpirit, takes the rice of al his motions from his passions, from the instigations of the Devil, and from the attractive baits of the world, which hurry him on to the pursuit of unlawful pleasures and satisfactions; and for a while drencht in these, he hugs himself in the enjoyment, as if they were his final end.

Thus it appears how inexcusable we are if we miss of our glorious final end, since it depends upon ourselves: nay to deviate from it we must even use violence, and check our natural inclination; we must becom our own enemy, ungrateful to our Creator, thwart our reason, forfeit al our glorious pretensions, and break throu al these chains to undo ourselves. O what infatuation? That man who is Lord of the univers, enriched, with reason, adorn'd with beauty, even to perfection, that he might be as it were a miracle to the rest of creatures here beneath, should be thrown down from al these prerogatives, quit a sovereign good to becom a slave to unruly passions, rais'd in him by sin.

Now the best preservative in this our tottering condition is, never to do any thing rashly, but first consider whether it conduces to our supernatural and blessed end; if so, then let our free wil embrace it; if otherwise, let the same noble faculty reject it, as a thing unlawful, and unworthy our immortal Being. So that steering our actions by the impuls of our free wil joynd with grace, which is never denied to the humble suppliant, we may attain to our beatitude with a ful satisfaction; for doubtles when we shal arrive at that state of Bliss, the reflection that we have don som thing in som little measure by the concurrence of our free wil in order to its acquisition, wil prove no smal ingredient to our contentment.

THE PRAYER.

O God, *who hast given to man a heart more capacious than*

the whole world, and in his Creation allotted to him for his portion celestial glory, let me not perish by a stupid ignorance of what I am and may be: but enable me with your grace always to correspond with the greatnes of my birth-right; and never yield to the childish baits of flesh and bloud, so far as to blemish my pretensions, or in the least hazard my eternal inheritance. Enlighten me to distinguish between eternal and temporal interests: that I may not pursue a shadow of happiness, and forfeit the substance of a real felicity, which is not found but in you my God by obeying your holy commands, for to their exact performance is annexed the promise of a life eternaly happy. Amen.

X. A MEDITATION

ON MAN'S BEATITUDE.

THat object which is capable to beatifie man ought to contain within it self al perfections, and univerfally whatever is good: for if deficient in the least, that defect will render a foul unsatisfied. Besides, it must communicate this plenitude in such manner as not to be exposed to any shadow of danger that it may be ravisht from her, for the want of this security will keep her always in suspense, and give a check to her compleat happiness: hence we may conclude, that no created object having a vertue without limit or change, consequently it belongs only to God who is infinit, and that he alone can lay the heart of man at rest, and glut al his desires.

REFLEXION.

In Beatitude al our desires are accomplish't.

Saint Austin says that there is a mutual enterchange between God and the blessed; God does possess the blessed as his peculiar and appropriated good; the blessed God, as their proper inheritance; and together with him they possess al other things: for earthly indowments are separate, power is not beauty, beauty is not knowledg, and the like; but in heaven you have whatever is great, or good, or pleasant, that can enter into mans imagination, and altogether at once without succession: for in eternity there is no past nor future, al is wrapt up in the present: if one sense here be recreated, and we intent upon it, the other senses have no satisfaction from their pleasing objects (thô applied unto them) for want of attention; but 'tis not so in heaven, our beatitude consists in the operation of the understanding, which is of a greater Capacity then the Organs of our senses, and consequently can deliciate it self in a thousand different objects at the same time, and so intimately, that as iron red hot seems to divest it self of its own form to put on that of fire; so God wil penetrate al the faculties of our soul as if she had lost her own Being, and becom one with him, so that our hearts wil be at rest; Conformably to which S. Austin says, God wil be the accomplishment of al our desires, Eternally to be seen, and unweariedly to be loved. Eternally to be seen, because by a clear vision the blessed wil be inseparably united unto God as their center, and sovereign good, which once attaind, they have nothing more to wish or desire : Vnweariedly to be loved, because he is an Ocean of delights, an inexhausted spring of perfections, stil creating a fresh appetite to behold and love him. Saint Gregory says the Angels behold God and desire to behold him, they thirst to behold him, even while they behold him: that is, their appetit is never cloy'd, and their desires never slacken'd, nor abated; both satiety and desire being joynd together. So that celestial beatitude admits nothing of relenting, but perfectly quiets al our pretentions. Our soul (says the Royal Prophet) which is as it were an Abyss of infinit capacity, cals and pants after God who is an Abyss of infinit greatnes, and who alone can replenish al her desires.

There are three propertyes attend Beatitude, the which settle a Soul alwayes in a perfect calm, and tranquillity. One is that she is impeccable, secure from the least deviation or sinful trespass. This innocence springs from the condition of Beatitude incompatible with sin : for a oul that hath a cleer vision of

God, beholds him so beautiful, so majestuous, so accomplishd in al perfection, that she would not hazard the loss for millions of worlds, besides to this vision is alwayes joynd an ardent affection, and if S. Paul amidst the miseryes of this life defyed al Beings whatsoever to separate him from the charity of JESUS CHRIST, much more in the state of Glory (which is free from al contest) may the blessed defye any to separate them from God: and thó our wil in heaven retain the possession of her liberty, or free choice, yet t'is there confined to what is good, and by consequence secures a soul from the least fear of sin, and settles her in a perfect peace and tranquillity.

The next property of Beatitude is, that a soul is embellishd with a beauty ineffable : for if a glorifyed body outstrips the Sun in splendour, much more wil the soul be illustrated by the light of glory, as also by her own glory consummated, vvhich vvil beautify her even to admiration, and immediately dispose her to contemplate, and unite herself to the infinit beautyes of her Creatour : for if grace here in this our pilgrimage irradiates a soul to that degree as her splendour is insupportable to a mortal eye, by the testimony of S. Bridget in her revelations, doubtless the light of glory vvhich is the perfection of grace vvil much add to her lustre. If then vve covet so much to have our bodys here adornd, if here vve are so passionat after a beauty that resembles a shadovv, more fleeting then the clouds, tarnisht vvith every little feaver and totally ruind by time, ah vvhy do vve not rather pant after Beatitude, vvhose charms are alvvaies vigourous, amiable, and renders us in al circumstances compleatly happy.

The third property is that its joyes wil be eternal this our happy end, wil be without end: for it consists in the vision, and love of God, which two operations

tions wil never cease; for God never withdrawes his gifts from Creatures unless upon something of demerit on their side, now as to this they are secured being raised above the activity of any natural Agent which may any wayes cause a prejudice to them. Lastly the soul wil not deprive herself of this her happiness, for she beholds nothing in God that is not most perfect, and ravishing, for in him she enjoyes a ful repose, abundance of satisfaction, and a delicious assurance of a glorious life for eternity.

In the primitive times Christians were usually styled disciples of heaven, and were so
m

...lations... ...ted from worldly glory ... they held it a different to their divine ma[ster] who had read to them ...me maximes of Eternal fe[licit]y) not to be eager in the [pu]rsuit of celestial glory. Nay he that appear'd to covet the hungry Elements of this world, so Saint Paul terms honor, wealth, and sensual pleasures, they proclaim'd an ingrate, that hat forgot the price of his Redemption: for Christ first open'd to us a passage unto heaven: next he purchased grace by which we are enabled to its acquisition. Lastly he taught us in our Pater noster daily to petition for that rich inheritance, *ing*, *thy Kingdom com*: yet alas man attends so little to these gracious blessings, at it occasioned Saint Austin to lament with a kind of admiration, that man kind for the most part should rather seek his felicity in a world deficient then in a God al-sufficient.

There is no rational Agent that having propos'd to him self an end, does not likewise pitch upon som means to arrive to this end. And these means ought also to have som proportion to the end. Now we am at Beatitude which is to Charm and allay al our desires: the means to compas this should be fitted with som quality which tends and leans towards quiet; and certainly a vertuous and holy life does most contribute to this end. For the beatitude of Saints is a sacred repose, and delicious banquet, a joy and undisturbed peace. So the just here upon earth are replenisht with grace, which is the seed of glory, and this occasions unto them a perfect tranquillity of mind; and their passions being reduced to a wondrous calm, they are deliciated whith a perpetual feast: every motion of their heart in pursuit of one and the same object, which being infinit, ansvvers to al their longings. Nay vve read of holy persons vvho have been overwhelmd with such a torrent of delights, that had they not been moderated, they must needs have made a paſſage unto death. Hence tis evident that a life of sanctity is a reſemblance that approaches the neereſt to a ſtate of bliſs, and may juſtly be termd the beatitude of this mortal life.

THE PRAYER.

O *God, before whoſe glorious throne, the ſeraphins and al the bleſſed in heaven bow down their flaming heads; adoring your greatnes, admiring your divine attributes, and raviſht with eternal affections, do inceſſantly chant forth* your praise: Grant to us your poor servants here under tryal that we may imitate in som little measure your celestial Chorists, paying our awful respects, by acts of adoration: Our obedience, by a perfect observance of your holy laws: Our love, by a pure sacrifice of al we are and have, to your sacred wil and pleasure: And as the sun passes over ordure without infecting its Rays; may we in like manner pass throu the sordid baits of this world until we arrive at thee our ô Center and sovereign good, after which al motions and pretensions wil end in eternal repose.   Amen.

THAT BEATITUDE

ADMITS NO GRIEF OR SADNES.

O What comfort to consider beatitude, which S. Austin defines in few words, a joy of truth, because God is the source of al verities: and in him we shal behold the wonders of our faith unvail'd: those divine mysteries which surpass al imagination wil be drawn out of obscurity into light, and strangely regale our understanding, causing ineffable joy within us; as to contemplate the divine productions, how the Son is coeternal

and confubstantial with the father, and how both by a mutual love breath forth the Holy Ghost, in al things equal to the father and the Son: to have the myftery of the holy Euchariſt unfolded to us, hovv God is pleafd to contract himfelf vvithin the compas of a fmal hoſt and to be grafp'd by our unvvorthy hands. To contemplate the vvonders of his providence in the governmét of this vvorld, hovv his divine vvifdom has fo managed the different events of human actions as to make of them a harmony of his glory: nay out of the clashing, and thvvarting malice of men, to dravv forth good. This cleer
pro-

prospect wil ravish the blessed, for as the sun enlightens a body by the instrument of the eyes, so God recreates and beatifies a soul by the understanding fortified with the light of glory: now to this joy which springs from the understanding succeeds a joy in the wil: and by how much the knowledg of a taking object is perfect, in proportion the wil embraces and loves it; for the understanding and wil are conducts by which joy is conveyd unto us; nay indeed the very flower, and fruit of joy. Hence as the blessed by the understanding contemplate the Divine Essence, face to face, without

any interpos'd vail, so the wil
Enflam'd from this prospect unites it self by a love ineffable unto God the fountain of al good. Thus the soul by these two faculties united to the most sovereign ād perfect object wil be plung'd in an Ocean of delights, and like a sponge be replenish'd on al sides with joy and exultation.

REFLEXION.

No true joy upon Earth.

Saint Austin ruminating upon the joy of the blessed, cried out, O joy above al joy, without which there is no joy; nay he pursues his transport saying, that to posses this joy for the space of one day, is more to be valued then the most exquisit pleasure of this world for innumerable years: but whilst our thoughts are entertaind with reflections on the joys of heaven, methinks tis a kind of solecism to name sadnes or grief: since the least exhalation of any discontent is for ever banisht that blessed Region: but as a black sets of, and adds lustre to a rare beauty, so a glance of our condition here beneath, wil render more pretious that blessed state exempt from al misery.

Know therefore in the first place that the goods of this

world are allotted to us for use, not for enjoyment: so that by a mistake in the tenour of the grant, we pervert the orders of our Creator, making that the subject of our enjoyment which is only designed for the convenience of our wel being: hence in reality there is no pleasure or satisfaction upon earth which affords a true and compleat joy. First by reason the nature of what is matter of our joy here is fleeting: next the changeablenes of our own humour, which is apt to dote upon this satisfaction to day, to morrow cloyd with it is passionately transported in the pursuit of another: lastly in that the conclusion of these contentments is for the most part heel'd with repentance: so that tis clear where their is no stability nor security in the matter of our joy, there must needs be either an apprehension of losing it, or wearines in the enjoyment, and consequently no true joy in the possession.

Besides, man is composed of different parts, by the one he is equalled with Angels, by the other rank'd amongst beasts: now all the pleasures of our sensual part are distastful to our spiritual substance: and since most of our delights are such, in proportion they give a check to our rational part: and by consequence the joy arising from those satisfactions is very imperfect. Ambition which aspires after honour and greatnes, is pleased with bended knees, applause of men, and the like: now al these beget no joy in a truly wise man, because the glories of his soul (which alone merit respect) are invisible, and above al the titles of honor the world can give. The satisfaction also which springs from carnal pleasures is much abated by our reason, that looks upon them as too low for an immortal being: the same of al other earthly contentments.

 Hence I wonder not that Saint Austin admiring Gods

wisdom in the conſtitution of this world should cry out : O what infelicity of mankind, the world is bitter, yet beloved, how, if pleaſant, would it be doted on : the world is ful of diſturbance, yet beloved, what would it be in peace and quiet? how would they gather its flowers when now its thorns cannot ſtop their hand ? upon this ground he gives a notable caution to beware of the world's ſmiles, and that we are never more in danger then vvhen we appear to be its darlings, by which you may ſee beſides that the world has no true joy its very ſeming joy is dangerous. That we may then arrive at

(200)

the fountain of true joy, let us joyn issue vvith this great experieced Saint, vvho assures that the best expedient to Elude al its snares are tears, sorrow and penitential acts. In pursuance Saint Bernard says, *O Good Jesu, if it be so svveet a thing to vveep for you, what vvil it be to rejoyce vvith you?* wherefore when the blessed shal look back into this depraved and corrupted world, a Chaos of confusion, a place orespread with nets of temptations, and cluttered vvith impediments of salvation, and that by Gods assisting grace they are dravvn offclear from al its hazards, and miseries, O vvhat vvings vvil this add to their joy? what incentives to spend themselves in the parfume of praise, and becom a perpetual sacrifice of thanksgiving for their consummated Glory.

THE PRAYER.

O God, Thou sage ruler of al things who in the establishment of your great family in this inferior world, hast ordaind the earth for our hope and heaven for our enjoyment: grant that I may never swil my self in the puddle of Earthly pleasures, but stil thirst after those pure refreshments reserved for us in the possession of Beatitude, where a ful draught wil be reacht to us from the fountain of al delights; where our tears shal be converted into pearls to adorn our Crowns; our sighs and groans, into the melody of Angels, and our pious sadnes and grief rise up into endles Jubilies. Amen.

FINIS.

APPROBATIO.

Cum Vir eximiè Doctus mihi declaraverit, librum cui titulus sequens appositus est, *Pious Reflections and devout prayers upon several points of Faith and morality, from Man's Creation to his consummation*, Nihil continere nisi conforme Sanæ Doctrinæ & bonis moribus, permitto ut Imprimatur. Datum Duaci Die 20 Maii. 1695.

NICOLAUS JOSEPHUS DE LA VERDURE, S. Theologiæ Doctor, & Professor Primarius.

Printed in the United States
101840LV00003B/220/A